Sorry, I don't speak English

The ACE project
'Literacy for active citizenship' series

Written by Nazma Shaheen
& Tinhinane Cheloul
Illustrations by Karen Dudley

Sorry, I don't speak English
© Learning Unlimited 2014

Published by Learning Unlimited Ltd as part of the Active Citizenship and Literacy (ACE) project. The ACE project led by Learning Unlimited, was funded through the European Integration Fund and delivered in partnership with Blackfriars Settlement, Working Men's College and the Institute of Education.

Foreword

The ACE project
'Literacy for active citizenship' series

The Active Citizenship and English (ACE) project, led by Learning Unlimited and delivered in partnership with Blackfriars Settlement, Working Men's College and the Institute of Education, received funding from the European Integration Fund (July 2013 to June 2015).

The ACE project aimed to support non-EU women to develop their skills and confidence in English as well as the knowledge and confidence to take an active part in everyday life in the UK. As part of the project we wanted to produce a series of readers for our learners, and other adults also settling in the UK, which include stories about funny, personal and less typical aspects of everyday life in the UK. These books were written by learners and volunteers on the ACE project and the supporting activities have been developed by the Learning Unlimited team.

We hope you enjoy using the 'Literacy for active citizenship' series.

To find out more about the ACE project, please see:
www.learningunlimited.co/projects/ace

Halima comes from Bangladesh and she
speaks Sylheti. She arrived in London
two weeks ago. She came to join her
husband. He is helping her to learn English.

A few days ago Halima went to her first
ESOL class. She felt excited and nervous
at the same time. She was also very worried
and asked herself a lot of questions.

"How do I introduce myself?

How will I know what to do?

Do I shake hands with the teacher?

How do I greet the other students?

What will the teacher ask me to say?

Where will I sit?

Who will I sit with?"

Halima arrived in class. She was very
surprised that her teacher was a man.
He smiled and said, "Hello". She said
hello and waited.

He pointed to a chair and said,
"Why don't you sit over there?"
Halima sat down and looked around.
She did not look at the teacher because
she felt shy.

The teacher asked Halima, "What's your name?" Her husband taught her the answer to this question so she answered, "My name is Halima." Then the teacher asked her another question. She didn't understand the question so she replied, "Sorry, I don't speak English." Everyone laughed!

The teacher asked another student to sit next to Halima. The other student's name was Nazma and she came from Bangladesh too.

Nazma helped Halima to understand what the teacher was saying and what to do in the class. Halima felt very happy and they soon became very good friends.

Key words

worried	think something is a problem
introduce herself	tell people who she is
greet	say hello

Activities

For downloadable activities, visit:
www.learningunlimited.co/resources/publications

Questions

1. Where does Halima come from?

2. How did she feel before her first ESOL class?

3. How did she feel at the end of her first ESOL class?

4. Why was Halima surprised when she saw her teacher?

5. How did you feel when you arrived in the UK?

6. How did you feel when you went to your first ESOL class? Were you worried?

7. Do you feel worried now when you go to a new class?

8. Do you think that it's important to go to ESOL classes to learn English? Why?

Acknowledgements

Sorry, I don't speak English was written by Nazma Shaheen and Tinhinane Cheloul and illustrated by Karen Dudley. We are grateful to them for being able to include their work as part of the 'Literacy for active citizenship' series.

To find out more about Learning Unlimited, its resources and published materials, CPD and teacher training programmes, project and consultancy work, please see: **www.learningunlimited.co**